AXIS PARENT GUIDES SERIES

A Parent's Guide to the Sex Talk

A Parent's Guide to Pornography

A Parent's Guide to Sexual Assault

A Parent's Guide to Suicide & Self-Harm Prevention

A Parent's Guide to Depression & Anxiety

PARENT GUIDE BUNDLES

Parent Guides to Social Media

Parent Guides to Finding True Identity

Parent Guides to Mental & Sexual Health

A PARENT'S GUIDE TO

PORN-OGRAPHY

Tyndale House Publishers
Carol Stream, Illinois

Visit Tyndale online at tyndale.com.

Visit Axis online at axis.org.

Tyndale and Tyndale's quill logo are registered trademarks of Tyndale House Ministries.

A Parent's Guide to Pornography

Copyright © 2023 by Axis. All rights reserved.

Cover illustration by Lindsey Bergsma. Copyright © Tyndale House Ministries. All rights reserved.

Designed by Lindsey Bergsma

Scripture quotations are taken from the Holy Bible, *New International Version,*® *NIV.*® Copyright © 1973, 1978, 2011 by Biblica, Inc.® Used by permission. All rights reserved worldwide.

For information about special discounts for bulk purchases, please contact Tyndale House Publishers at csresponse@tyndale.com, or call 1-855-277-9400.

Library of Congress Cataloging-in-Publication Data

A catalog record for this book is available from the Library of Congress.

ISBN 978-1-4964-6758-4

Printed in the United States of America

29	28	27	26	25	24	23
7	6	5	4	3	2	1

Pornography is a social toxin
that destroys relationships, steals
innocence, erodes compassion,
breeds violence, and kills love.

**PORNOGRAPHY AND PUBLIC HEALTH:
RESEARCH SUMMARY BY THE
NATIONAL CENTER ON SEXUAL
EXPLOITATION**

CONTENTS

A LETTER FROM AXIS

Dear Reader,

We're Axis, and since 2007, we've been creating resources to help connect parents, teens, and Jesus in a disconnected world. We're a group of gospel-minded researchers, speakers, and content creators, and we're excited to bring you the best of what we've learned about making meaningful connections with the teens in your life.

This parent's guide is designed to help start a conversation. Our goal is to give you enough knowledge that you're able to ask your teen informed questions about their world. For each guide, we spend weeks reading, researching, and interviewing parents and teens in order to distill everything you need to know about the topic at hand. We encourage you to read the whole thing and then to use the questions we include to get the conversation going with your teen—and then to follow the conversation wherever it leads.

As Douglas Stone, Bruce Patton, and Sheila Heen point out in their book *Difficult Conversations*, "Changes in attitudes and behavior rarely come about because of arguments, facts, and attempts to persuade. How often do *you* change your values and beliefs—or whom you love or what you want in life—based on something someone tells you? And how likely are you to do so when the person who is trying to change you doesn't seem fully aware of the reasons you see things differently in the first place?"[1] For whatever reason, when we believe that others are trying to understand *our* point of view, our defenses usually go down, and we're more willing to listen to *their* point of view. The rising generation is no exception.

So we encourage you to ask questions, to listen, and then to share your heart with your teen. As we often say at Axis, discipleship happens where conversation happens.

Sincerely,
Your friends at Axis

---

[1] Douglas Stone, Bruce Patton, and Sheila Heen, *Difficult Conversations: How to Discuss What Matters Most*, rev. ed. (New York: Penguin Books, 2010), 137.

IF WE DON'T DISCIPLE OUR KIDS ABOUT SEXUALITY, PORN WILL DO IT FOR US

THERE ARE FEW CULTURAL ISSUES more pressing than the problem of pornography. Though extremely damaging to us, porn appeals to powerful urges that God created as good. Sexually explicit material has always been a cultural pitfall, but the internet and smartphones have provided unprecedented access to it.

Meanwhile, the nature of porn and our cultural attitudes toward it have shifted significantly over the past several decades. Material that was once considered pornographic is now almost quaint. And while it's refreshing that various popular celebrities are speaking out about the destructive nature of porn[1], society as a whole has widely accepted pornography as normal and/or healthy.

This guide focuses on the general problem of porn in our culture. Know from the outset that you might find some of the information in this guide disturbing. We have done our best to include only what we think you need to know to be aware of the extent of the problem of porn so that you can more effectively guide your family and cultivate deeper conversations.

While it's refreshing that various popular celebrities are speaking out about the destructive nature of porn, society as a whole has widely accepted pornography as normal and/or healthy.

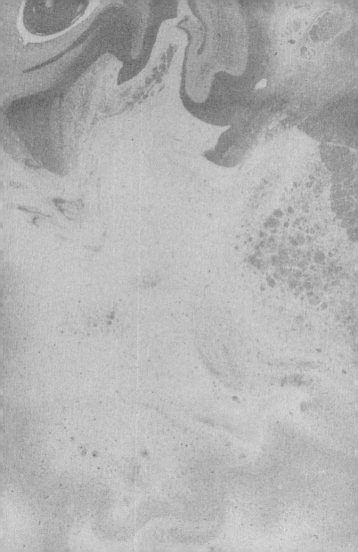

WHAT'S PORN LIKE THESE DAYS?

PORN TAKES COUNTLESS FORMS, but *Merriam-Webster* provides a simple yet accurate definition: "the depiction of erotic behavior (as in pictures or writing) intended to cause sexual excitement."[2] If we sift through our culture looking for imagery or content that is designed to make people think about sex, then it's fairly obvious that our culture is becoming increasingly "pornified." That is, qualities and behaviors that have been typically associated with porn are becoming more and more acceptable in mainstream culture.

The National Center on Sexual Exploitation (NCSE) observes:

> The pornification of culture (i.e. softcore, hypersexualized imagery) is widespread and evident everywhere, from the grocery store checkout lane to advertising,

popular entertainment, unsolicited email, and beyond. It's becoming increasingly difficult—if not impossible—to live a porn-free life.[3]

While the above definition seems fairly straightforward, today's teens and young adults likely have a blurry definition of what exactly porn is. For example, people have traditionally referred to porn as being either "softcore" or "hardcore," and to some extent this terminology still holds. But in the documentary *Over 18*, anti-porn activist and sociology professor Gail Dines observes that this distinction is becoming less and less relevant.[4]

Softcore porn typically refers to partial or full nudity and "suggestive" situations, whereas hardcore porn refers to graphic depictions of sex, including intercourse.

But now, what people in past eras would have understood as being softcore porn has simply become part of our culture. Modern pornography is hardcore by definition. So whereas older genera-tions likely perceive *Playboy*, *Hustler*, and *Penthouse* as pornographic, newer gen-erations of porn users might not think of these magazines as being pornographic at all. The *mainstream* pornography that people encounter now includes depic-tions of things like aggressive anal sex or scenes where three men have sex with a woman simultaneously.

If today's teens and young adults perceive softcore porn as normal, they are likely consuming pornographic content in their media without recognizing it as such. And the rest of us might not be aware of how the norms of porn are influencing our culture. For example, in November

2019, fashion magazine *Teen Vogue* ran an article instructing readers on how to have anal sex.[5] And while it's long been common for male musical artists to objectify women in their songs, now female artists are objectifying men and other women. We've transitioned from a time when networks wouldn't air a TV show depicting couples sleeping in the same bed to a time when the most popular shows contain graphic nudity (e.g., HBO's highly popular *Game of Thrones* or the Netflix show *Altered Carbon*).

WHAT DO TEENS AND YOUNG ADULTS THINK ABOUT PORN?

A FEW YEARS AGO, JOSH MCDOWELL partnered with Barna Group to do a study called "The Porn Phenomenon." They discovered a key generational difference in how people see porn use—namely, that younger people for the most part view it as normal.

Teens and young adults are living in an environment where porn is more acceptable—and more ubiquitous than ever before. As access to pornography has increased, the stigma toward it has seemingly decreased. There is just a general assumption that people are using porn—especially among teens and young adults. And this assumption is not a negative one. When it comes to watching pornography, teens and young adults aren't getting accountability from their friends—they are getting peer pressure.[6]

Barna found that *young people are much more likely to see failing to recycle as more morally reprehensible than using porn.* On average, only 16 percent of Christians are actively trying to stop using porn, compared to 9 percent of non-Christians.[7]

The porn industry's revenue and online traffic tell us a lot about how much people are viewing porn. It's a global industry that nets billions of dollars per year worldwide.[8] About 12 percent of all websites are pornographic,[9] 25 percent of web searches are pornographic,[10] and tens of millions of cases of child pornography are reported each year.[11]

"When it comes to watching pornography, teens and young adults aren't getting accountability from their friends—they are getting peer pressure." [They] are much more likely to see failing to recycle as more morally reprehensible than using porn.

—BARNA

WHERE DO PEOPLE FIND PORN?

THE DAYS OF KIDS SEEKING OUT and sneaking in smutty magazines are long gone. Instead, pornography is out to find them. Online porn is obviously a huge concern for parents, but let's not forget about the other ways kids can encounter it.

Many people unintentionally come across online porn through pop-ups and ads. Some encounter it through receiving and opening a link that they were not aware went to a pornographic site.[12] Certain video games contain pornographic content (and even "safe" video games might show explicit ads).[13] A child could accidentally access porn when searching on Google for something else.

One woman we talked to saw a graphic image on Twitter simply because a pornographic account followed her and had that image in its profile. She blocked and reported the account, but she had already seen the image simply because that user followed her. Users of Instagram have reported that searching "#california" on that platform brought up images of nudity. Snapchat is another problematic social media platform because their Stories feature often promotes sexual content (e.g., cleavage "battles" between celebrities).

And yes, kids can still encounter porn offline, such as through cable TV or magazines. If your kids' friends have access to porn somehow, your children might be exposed through them. The organization Defend Young Minds lists several situations in which porn might find kids unaware, as well as measures parents can take to protect their children in those situations.[14] A few notable scenarios are:

- Grandparents' house

- Sleepovers

- The school bus

- While babysitting

We think it's worth noting the most common avenues through which people are currently seeking out porn. Pornhub (the largest porn site on the internet) has an exhaustive list of statistics about its users in its Year in Review. (Warning: Pornhub stats are not explicit, but they are on the Pornhub domain and are still very disturbing.)

Almost 77 percent of porn viewed on this site in 2019 was via phone. Computers (desktop and laptop) now comprise less than 17 percent of Pornhub's traffic. The most popular browser for viewing porn on Pornhub is Google Chrome. Pornhub also notes how much traffic it got through gaming consoles such as Nintendo, Xbox, and PlayStation. *Please note* that if you have internet filtering software for your computers and smartphones but have neglected your gaming consoles, these are potential inlets for porn.

Please note that if you have internet filtering software for your computers and smartphones but have neglected your gaming consoles, these are potential inlets for porn.

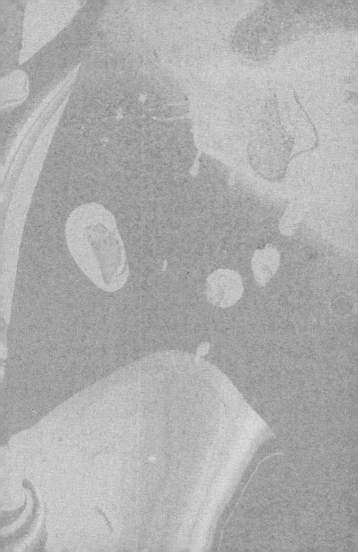

WHEN DO PEOPLE ENCOUNTER PORN?

PEOPLE DISAGREE SLIGHTLY about the average age of exposure to pornography. The creators of *Over 18* cite it as age twelve, noting that this means that for every fifteen-year-old who is exposed, a nine-year-old is exposed as well. Others put the average age at eleven,[15] while some say it is as young as seven.[16] Whether or not seven is the actual average age, seven-year-olds are most certainly at risk of finding porn.

Almost all men and a majority of women are exposed to porn by the time they are adults. In 2008, a study of 560 college students found that 62 percent of girls and 93 percent of boys encountered porn by the time they were eighteen (and that was over a decade ago!).[17] Defend Young Minds says 10 percent of visitors to porn sites are younger than ten years old.[18] Covenant Eyes reports that 64 percent of men and 15 percent of women who are self-identified Christians look at porn at least once a month.[19] Sadly, it's rarer for people in Generation Z (those born around or after the turn of the century) not to have seen porn than to have seen it.[20]

HOW DOES PORN AFFECT USERS?

SADLY, BUT NOT SURPRISINGLY, porn does an incredible amount of damage to its users and to those around them. Researchers have linked porn to mental health issues, antisocial behavior, and abuse.[21] It even causes changes in the brain, following the same patterns as other addictive substances.[22] Porn has also been linked to sexual dysfunction and decreased sexual satisfaction.

Research has shown that porn makes people more aggressive, narcissistic, and misogynistic. People who consume porn are less likely to marry and less likely to seek out sexual consent from their partners. They are more prone to be unfaithful to their partners and more likely to commit sexual crimes.[23]

Researchers have linked porn to mental health issues, antisocial behavior, and abuse. It even causes changes in the brain, following the same patterns as other addictive substances.

WHAT'S THE RELATIONSHIP BETWEEN PORN AND SEX TRAFFICKING?

IT'S NOT UNUSUAL FOR A YOUNG PERSON today to be outraged by human trafficking, while at the same time seeing porn use as perfectly acceptable. But the truth is that porn and sex trafficking are inextricably linked.

Some people argue that porn allows them to have sexual release without involving another person, making porn a "safer" alternative to acting out sexually with someone in real life. But research shows the opposite. People who use porn are actually more prone to purchase the services of prostitutes. According to the NCSE,

> An analysis of 101 sex buyers
> compared to 100 men who did
> not buy sex found that sex buyers
> masturbate to pornography
> more often than non–sex buyers,
> masturbate to more types of

pornography, and reported that
their sexual preferences changed
so that they sought more
sadomasochistic and anal sex.
Other research also demonstrates
an association between purchase
of commercial sex acts and
pornography use.[24]

In fact, porn users are four times more
likely to patronize prostitutes.[25] Prostitutes
themselves report that clients request
that they enact explicit scenes their clients have viewed. There is also a direct
connection between porn use and violence against prostitutes.[26]

Additionally, an article discussing prostitution and trafficking states, "Pornography
may meet the legal definition of trafficking to the extent that the pornographer
recruits, entices, or obtains the people

depicted in pornography for the purpose of photographing commercial sex acts."[27]

Pornography can sometimes be the recorded evidence of sex trafficking, as well as directly fuels the demand for exploitation and sex trafficking. Even worse, it's estimated that about 1 in 5 pornographic images online is of a minor.[28] In 2018, giant tech companies reported over 45 million photos and videos of child sexual abuse on their platforms.[29]

Cappatt also noted that there is no way to know whether a porn actor or actress is participating voluntarily or was forced or pressured into doing so. Atlas Free reported an instance where a major porn star was in fact a victim of human trafficking, and the people creating the film were not aware of it.

HOW DO PEOPLE RATIONALIZE USING PORN?

"IT'S PRIVATE, SO IT'S NOT HURTING ANYONE."

One of the most common justifications by far is that because porn use is private, it's not hurting anyone. We disagree with the underlying assumption in that statement, which is that actions are right or wrong based solely on whether we believe they will hurt others. We might not be able to see the damage our actions are causing, but real harm could still be occurring.

For example, we could indulge in lust in our hearts and say it's fine because we're not acting on our desires by having an affair. But whether we recognize it or not, that sin still impacts every part of our lives, such as our ability to worship God and be in healthy relationships with those closest to us. Our values should not simply be determined by what we think hurts people. They need to be rooted

We must base our morality on God's character, not on our subjective perceptions. Porn is objectively wrong because it violates God's character and the rules He gave to protect our flourishing.

in who God is: just, merciful, and loving. We must base our morality on God's character, not on our subjective perceptions. *Porn is objectively wrong because it violates God's character and the rules He gave to protect our flourishing.* As Pope John Paul II once said, "The problem with pornography is not that it shows too much of the person, but that it shows far too little."[30] God sees us as whole persons, not as objects, and He asks us to do the same.

And as we've already noted, porn *does* hurt its users. It makes them depressed, aggressive, and less empathetic toward others, and it has been linked to sexual dysfunction in both men and women. Porn is not merely an outlet for sexual desire, but an inlet as well. It increases people's sexual appetites and becomes less satisfying over time.

"THE ACTORS ARE PARTICIPATING VOLUNTARILY."

Whether or not male and female porn stars are participating voluntarily, to watch them is still to take part in their degradation and to treat them as less than human. As a comparison, when people willingly harm themselves, it's wrong for us to celebrate their harm. Even when sin is done voluntarily, it's still sin, and it's wrong for us to support it.

But again, porn users have no way of knowing whether or not the people—the actresses in particular—are participating voluntarily. A woman in a video might be willingly employed as a porn star, or she might be a victim of human trafficking.

Even if porn actresses are not being trafficked, it's more than possible they are being pressured into doing something they feel uncomfortable with but are

Porn only focuses on the physical aspect of sex and ignores the emotional, mental, and spiritual impact it has on those involved (which highlights the need for Christian parents to be more open and willing to teach their kids, starting at young ages, about healthy, God-honoring sex).

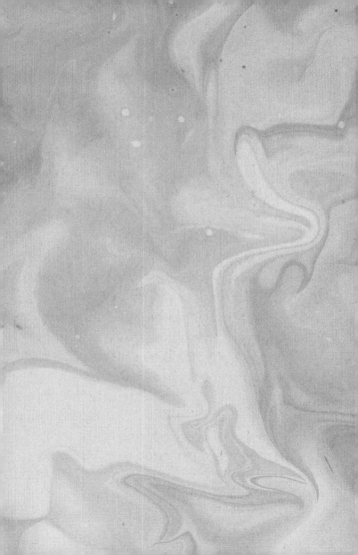

tolerating anyway. If you can, we recommend watching the *Over 18* documentary we referenced earlier. It provides a glimpse into the effects of the industry on two female porn stars who were very popular at one time and who joined the industry willingly.

"PORN IS EDUCATING ME ABOUT SEX."

Many people turn to porn to fill in gaps in their sexual education. But porn shows an exaggerated, unrealistic depiction of sex, something that people in the adult film industry admit themselves. In addition, porn only focuses on the physical aspect of sex and ignores the emotional, mental, and spiritual impact it has on those involved (which highlights the need for Christian parents to be more open and willing to teach their kids, starting at young ages, about healthy, God-honoring sex).

"IT'S FREE, SO I'M NOT SUPPORTING THE PORN INDUSTRY."

It's easy to see how someone would think this is true, but it most definitely is not. When people watch porn, whether it's free or not, they support the industry by fueling the demand for porn, increasing its online traffic and popularity—and therefore its profits.[31] So even people who don't pay for porn online are supporting the industry in a real way.

CAN'T I JUST BLOCK ALL PORN USING STRONG FILTERS?

Filters do close the floodgates and make porn harder to access . . . But no filter is an adequate substitute for parents talking often and openly about pornography and its lies.

IF A COMPUTER HAS NO INTERNET FILTERS, all someone has to do to watch porn is type "porn" (or "naked" or "boobs" or similar terms) into any search engine. It's a free-for-all. So yes, filters do close the floodgates and make porn harder to access—and make it less likely that younger kids will stumble across something sexual that they can't understand. *But no filter is an adequate substitute for parents talking often and openly about pornography and its lies.*

Certain internet filters are more effective than others at blocking porn. Look for filters that can handle HTTPS sites, are browser independent, and will not be fooled by anonymous proxies. If you have internet-aware devices that you can't install filtering software on, such as gaming consoles or iPods, we recommend OpenDNS Home, which has a solid free version that filters all devices connected to your network. We also like Covenant Eyes because of its focus on personal accountability, specifically when it comes to porn. But again, no matter what filters we opt for, we cannot rely solely on parental controls to protect our kids from porn.

If our children want to watch porn, they *will* find ways to get around our filters (check out the Defend Young Minds article "6 Ways Savvy Kids Can Circumvent Your Internet Controls" for more on this).[32] Even if they don't have any interest in porn, it's possible that porn might slip through the cracks, simply as a fluke or the result of human error. A child could accidentally encounter a pornographic magazine at a friend's house or be sent images through chat on a kid-friendly video game or on a chat platform such as Discord. We simply don't know where they might encounter it. Internet filters, while helpful, are not sufficient in and of themselves to combat this issue.

HOW DO KIDS HIDE PORN?

SOME PEOPLE HIDE PORNOGRAPHY on their computers by using misleading file names or by encrypting their files.[33] They might conceal porn by looking for it in a private browsing mode. They might save it on their devices by using an app designed to hide pictures.[34]

Another option for concealing online activity is using a virtual private network (VPN) or an anonymous browser such as TOR. Keep in mind that if your internet filter only filters your WiFi network, your kids could potentially bypass those restrictions by getting on your neighbor's network or on public WiFi, or by using cellular data.

HOW CAN I TELL IF MY KIDS ARE LOOKING AT PORN?

DEFEND YOUNG MINDS says there are several signs you can look for in your children's behavior to indicate that they might be viewing porn.[35]

- **Clearing their browser histories.** Clearing the history doesn't necessarily mean that your kids have been looking at porn, but it's worth looking into this suspicious behavior.

- **Spending a lot of time online at night.** In 2019, Pornhub found that the most common time its users viewed porn was between 10 p.m. and 12 a.m., and the most trafficked day of the week was Sunday. Even if your kids aren't looking at porn, being on their devices right before going to bed is a bad habit.

- **Spending a lot of time in the bathroom on their devices.** Really, if you see your kids shutting themselves off anywhere with their devices for periods of time, that's a warning sign.

- **Changing their screens when you come around.** Again, why would they need to do this unless they are trying to hide something?

- **Acting more moody, irritable, depressed, or aggressive.** Watch out for changes in your kids' behavior or a lack of interest in activities they used to love. Also be aware that porn can be a major factor in causing child-on-child sexual abuse.

WHAT CAN I DO TO PROTECT MY KIDS FROM PORN?

WE CAN'T SAY THIS ENOUGH: the most important step you can take as you raise your kids is to pray for them. We know of a mom who prayed that if her son were viewing porn, God would let her find out about it—which is exactly what happened.

Pursue relationships with your kids. Get to know them and build trust with them. Make sure they know how much you love them. If you invest in them, you earn the right to talk with them about personal issues like porn use. Psychologist Patricia M. Greenfield says, "A warm and communicative parent-child relationship is the most important non-technical means that parents can use [in reducing online porn use among children]."[36]

We need to have conversations with our kids about sex and porn early and often. We cannot afford to think we're going to

have "the talk" with them one time when
they're about ten years old. Many kids are
encountering porn before age ten.

The common argument against preparing
kids for encountering porn is that raising
the subject with them will make them curious and want to seek it out. It is possible
that bringing up the issue of porn could
make your kids curious about it. But you
can forestall this possibility by being wise
about how you have these conversations.

In their "SMART Guide for Parents,"
Defend Young Minds says the following
strategies will help prevent children from
seeking out information about porn on
their own:[37]

- Make sure they know you are
  completely open to any follow-up
  questions they have.

- Make sure they know the internet is a dangerous place to go looking for answers about porn.

- Regularly follow up with them on this topic.

- Have frequent family discussions about media safety.

The risk of our kids encountering porn is so great that if we remain silent about it, we surrender our opportunity to shape our kids' perspectives on sexuality. Instead, we allow our culture to do so. See Defend Young Minds' "5 Reasons You Should Initiate Your Kid's Curiosity about Porn (Before Someone Else Does!)" for more.[38]

So how do we prepare our children for encountering porn when they are too young to even understand what sex is? First, we can seek out resources such as

The risk of our kids encountering porn is so great that if we remain silent about it, we surrender our opportunity to shape our kids' perspectives on sexuality.

"How Christian Parents Can Talk to Their Children about Sex," an article from Seattle Christian Counseling that describes the typical sexual curiosity and behavior of children at different age levels so we can formulate appropriate strategies based on the age of our kids.[39]

Next, we must consider what we should do to protect our children from sexual predators. If they are old enough to talk and to understand what their private parts are, we can have a basic conversation with them about how no one should be touching them there. If someone does—or asks to— we have to make sure our children know to tell us immediately and not to be afraid that we'll be angry with them. However, the best way to protect them from physical predators is with our presence—and our knowledge of where they are when they are not in our presence.

It's quite possible to have similar conversations with younger children about the internet without being too explicit. If they ever see someone's private parts online, they need a strategy. Make sure they know to tell you and not to be afraid or ashamed. If they ever view something that scares or disturbs them, they can tell you about it. No strategy is fail-safe, but at least you can open the door to talking about pornography with your young children without being graphic. What's more, you can do so at an age when they're more open to talking to you than they will be in their teenage years.

As early as possible, we have to talk to our children about what healthy expressions of sexuality look like and educate them on the harmful consequences of porn. We need to start these conversations on some level as early as six to eight years old, if not sooner.[40] One tool you might look into for starting these discussions with your kids is the book *Good Pictures Bad Pictures Jr.* by Kristen A. Jenson, which is a resource for talking to kids ages three to six about porn in an age-appropriate way. Also, check out the article "The Hard-to-Have Conversations," a resource from the Australian government about how to talk to children about porn.[41]

When having these conversations—especially as our kids get older—it's crucial that *we* are willing to be vulnerable and sincere. If we haven't established trust with our kids and we wait to broach the topic of porn with them until they're already teenagers, it's extremely unlikely that they will be open with us. If they are viewing porn at that point, they will probably just lie to us about it.

It's easy to be tempted to hide our own failings so that we don't lose credibility with our kids. But being dishonest or inauthentic is what will actually cause us to lose credibility. None of us is immune to sexual temptation because none of us is immune to our fallen nature. Share about your weaknesses if your kids are old enough to understand. Your willingness to be open can be extremely powerful in helping them to listen to you. Your stories of overcoming temptation can also be a great encouragement. Communicate how much you love them and that you don't want them to be hurt.

When Queen Esther had a request to make of the Persian king that would affect all of the Jewish people, she and the Jews fasted and prayed for three days before she approached him (Esther 4:15-16). Take these conversations with your kids seriously enough that you prepare with prayer and even fasting, if you feel so led.

FINAL
THOUGHTS

CONVERSATION IS HUGE, but there is more we can do to protect our kids from porn. It's essential that we model healthy marriage for our kids whenever possible. Apart from culture, the main place they will get their vision for male-female relationships is from the example we set for them. We must also establish healthy boundaries, especially when it comes to technology, and seek out a community that provides accountability with vulnerability and trust. We can educate our children on the way porn impacts those who view it and teach them to care about the victims of the porn and sex-trafficking industries.

We could say much more on this sobering topic. Yet despite all the discouraging news out there about porn, Barna's editor in chief, Roxanne Stone, points us toward hope: "The porn phenomenon is not a time for apocalyptic and hysterical rhetoric, but an opportunity to advance the life-giving messages of the gospel."[42] The best tactic for overcoming the power of porn is offering the much better and more fulfilling vision for sex, sexuality, relationships, and flourishing that is found only through Christ. We have to give our children something better to strive for and work toward (real love, abundant life, healthy relationships, God's glory), not just tell them what to avoid (porn, lust, trafficking, exploitation, unfulfilling sex).

We are all sexually broken on some level, and God's grace *is* sufficient for *all* of our brokenness, no matter how deep it goes. If you are addressing this issue with your children, you are already miles ahead of many parents out there. Rely on the Father for your strength, and don't give up.

"The porn phenomenon is not a time for apocalyptic and hysterical rhetoric, but an opportunity to advance the life-giving messages of the gospel."

—ROXANNE STONE
(EDITOR IN CHIEF OF BARNA)

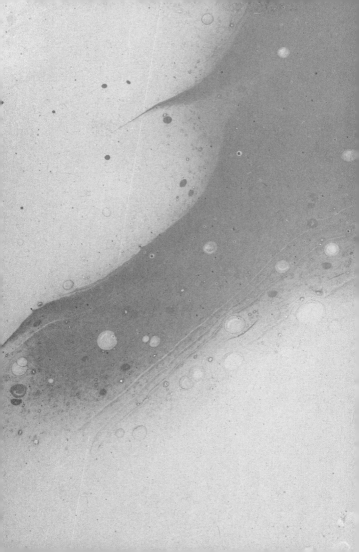

RECAP

- If we don't disciple our kids about sexuality, porn will.

- Teens and young adults are living in an environment where porn is more acceptable—and more ubiquitous—than ever before.

- Children are exposed to porn through magazines, online advertisements, friends and family, messaging and social media, and internet searches.

- Many kids are first exposed to pornography at ten years old or younger, and it's very rare for members of Gen Z not to be exposed to porn during their teen years.

- Porn affects the viewer, the actors and actresses, our families, and our society.

- Increased porn usage in society has led to an increase in sex trafficking.

- Even though people try to rationalize porn in many ways, there is no legitimate reason for Christians to look at porn.

- We should use internet filters to protect our kids, but we must also engage in difficult conversations with them.

- Our kids may try to hide porn from us, and we need to be aware of the telltale signs of porn usage.

- We need to talk with our kids about porn in age-appropriate ways, and we must have regular conversations about sexuality with openness and vulnerability.

- None of us is immune to sexual temptation, but we can have hope that our pornified culture is an opportunity to advance the life-giving messages of the gospel.

None of us is immune to sexual temptation, but we can have hope that our pornified culture is an opportunity to advance the life-giving messages of the gospel.

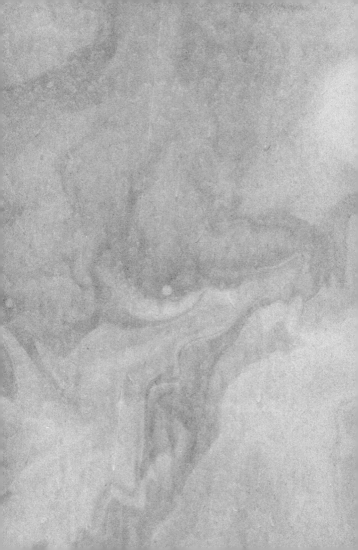

DISCUSSION QUESTIONS

1. How would you define porn? Do you think the average person is okay with consuming media that could be defined as pornographic?

2. Do you think porn is harmful? Do you think it's acceptable in any situation?

3. Many people think porn is okay because it's a way of getting sexual release without involving another person. What do you think about that?

4. Do you have any friends who use porn? Have you noticed that porn is affecting them in any way?

5. Have you ever seen porn online? If so, where? How did you react to it?

6. Do you feel like you can talk to me about this issue? Why or why not? How can I help you feel comfortable with approaching me?

7. Why is porn so appealing to people? What good part of God's creation is porn twisting and corrupting?

8. Do you believe that God's vision for sexuality is really more beautiful and desirable than porn's?

9. Can people struggle with lust without looking at porn? What does it look like to struggle with lust? How do you know if you've crossed the line from sexual attraction into lust?

10. People often masturbate while viewing porn. Is masturbation wrong? Why or why not?

11. What can you do to protect yourself from giving into lust or looking at porn? (Parents, this is likely a conversation best had between fathers/sons and mother/daughters if possible. We recommend that you be open about how you fight lust in your own life.)

ADDITIONAL RESOURCES

1. "The Terrible Cost of Porn," *American Conservative*, https://www.theamericanconservative.com/terrible-cost-of-porn/

2. Gail Dines, http://gaildines.com/

3. "Growing Up in a Pornified Culture" (strong language), TEDx Talk by Gail Dines, https://www.youtube.com/watch?v=_YpHNImNsx8

4. "How to Hide VR Porn on Your Gear VR," VRHeads, https://www.vrheads.com/how-hide-vr-porn-your-gear-vr

5. Fight the New Drug, https://fightthenewdrug.org/

6. Covenant Eyes blog, https://www.covenanteyes.com/blog/

7. Fortify, https://www.joinfortify.com/

8. Pure Desire Ministries, https://puredesire.org/

9. "The Hard-to-Have Conversations" and "The Effects of Pornography on Children and Young People," Australian Government, https://www.esafety.gov

.au/parents/skills-advice/hard-to-have
-conversations and https://aifs.gov.au
/research/research-snapshots/effects
-pornography-children-and-young
-people

10. "Resource Hub: Parents," Novus Project,
http://thenovusproject.org/resource-hub
/parents

11. Go for Greatness Facebook page, https://
www.facebook.com/greatnessorg/

12. The Protection Project: Journal of
Human Rights and Civil Society, Issue 5,
https://www.rescuefreedom.org/wp
-content/uploads/2017/10/slave-and-the
-porn-star.pdf

13. "Does the Porn Industry Use 'Tobacco
Industry Tactics' to Hide the Dark
Truth?" Fight the New Drug, https://
fightthenewdrug.org/porn-industry
-uses-tobacco-industry-tactics-to-hide
-the-truth/

14. The Porn Phenomenon: New Research
of Global Importance, Set Free Summit,
https://setfreesummit.org/barna-study/

15. "The Great Tech Panic: The Inevitability of Porn," *Wired*, https://www.wired.com/2017/08/kids-and-porn/

16. *Unwanted: How Sexual Brokenness Reveals Our Way to Healing*, Jay Stringer

17. *Rethinking Sexuality: God's Design and Why It Matters*, Juli Slattery

18. "How Pimps Recruit: Harmony's Story," Hope for the Sold, https://www.youtube.com/watch?v=un8iVJAwx8I

19. "When Your Kids Look at Porn," Authentic Intimacy, https://www.authenticintimacy.com/resources/8006/when-your-kids-look-at-porn

20. "Masturbation: Is It Wrong?" Authentic Intimacy, https://www.authenticintimacy.com/resources/6962/masturbation-is-it-wrong

21. "A Challenge from the Song of Solomon," Authentic Intimacy, https://www.authenticintimacy.com/resources/3303/a-challenge-from-the-song-of-solomon

22. "Sexual Discipleship®: What Is It, and Why Is It Important?" Authentic Intimacy, https://www.authenticintimacy.com /resources/2641/the-importance-of -sexual-discipleship

23. *The Heart of Man* (cinematic retelling of the Prodigal Son interwoven with true testimonials of personal and sexual brokenness), http://heartofmanmovie .com/

24. *Atomic Habits: An Easy & Proven Way to Build Good Habits & Break Bad Ones*, James Clear

NOTES

1. "12 Hollywood Stars Who Have Spoken Out on Porn's Harms," Fight the New Drug, August 12, 2022, https://fightthenewdrug.org/8-hollywood-stars-who-dont-watch-porn/.

2. "Pornography (n.)," Merriam-Webster, accessed September 22, 2022, https://www.merriam-webster.com/dictionary/pornography.

3. "Pornography & Public Health Research Summary," National Center on Sexual Exploitation, August 15, 2017, https://familywatch.org/wp-content/uploads/sites/5/2019/07/NCOSE_Pornography-Public-Health_RESEARCH-SUMMARY_8-15-17.pdf.

4. *Over 18*, directed by Jared Brock, IMDb, 2016, https://www.imdb.com/title/tt8031628/.

5. Gigi Engle, "Anal Sex: Safety, How Tos, Tips, and More," *Teen Vogue*, November 12, 2019, https://www.teenvogue.com/story/anal-sex-what-you-need-to-know.

6. "Porn in the Digital Age: New Research Reveals 10 Trends," Barna, April 6, 2016, https://www.barna.com/research/porn-in-the-digital-age-new-research-reveals-10-trends/.

7. "Porn in the Digital Age."

8. "Is the Porn Industry Worth Billions of Dollars?" Fight the New Drug, March 8, 2019, https://fightthenewdrug.org/how-free-porn-industry-growing-in-fast-paced-digitized/.

9. "Pornography Facts and Statistics," The Recovery Village, September 13, 2022, https://www.therecoveryvillage.com/process-addiction/porn-addiction/pornography-statistics/.

10. Robert Weiss, "The Prevalence of Porn," PsychCentral, May 22, 2013, https://psychcentral.com/blog/sex/2013/05/the-prevalence-of-porn#1.

11. Michael H. Keller and Gabriel J. X. Dance, "The Internet Is Overrun with Images of Child Sexual Abuse. What Went Wrong?" *New York Times*, September 29, 2019, https://www.nytimes.com/interactive/2019/09/28/us/child-sex-abuse.html.

12. Emily Kent Smith, "Youngsters as Young as 11 'Addicted' to Online Porn as 2,000 Children Seek Counselling Having Viewed Sickening Material While Surfing the Web," *Daily Mail*, March 15, 2018, https://www.dailymail.co.uk /news/article-5507751/NSPCC-offers-counselling-children-young-11-addicted -porn.html.

13. "Sexual Content in Video Games," Wikipedia, accessed September 22, 2022, https:// en.wikipedia.org/wiki/Sex_and_nudity _in_video_games.

14. Marilyn Evans, "5 Sneaky Locations Porn Finds Kids," Defend Young Minds, March 27, 2018, https://www.defendyoungminds.com/post /5-sneaky-locations-porn-finds-kids.

15. "The Detrimental Effects of Pornography on Small Children," Net Nanny, December 19, 2017, https://www.netnanny.com/blog/the -detrimental-effects-of-pornography-on -small-children/.

16. "What's the Average Age of a Child's First Exposure to Porn?" Fight the New Drug, April 21, 2022, https://fightthenewdrug.org/real -average-age-of-first-exposure/.

17. "Pornography Statistics," Covenant Eyes, accessed September 22, 2022, https://www .covenanteyes.com/pornstats/.

18. Kristen A. Jenson, "Kids under 10 Make Up 10% of Porn Site Visitors," Defend Young Minds, August 24, 2017, https://www.defend youngminds.com/post/one-in-ten-visitors -to-porn-sites-age-10-or-under.

19. "Pornography Statistics."

20. "10 Traits of Generation Z," Lifeway Research, September 29, 2017, https://research.lifeway .com/2017/09/29/10-traits-of-generation-z/.

21. "10 Negative Effects of Porn on Your Brain, Body, Relationships, and Society," Fight the New Drug, August 5, 2022, https://fightthe newdrug.org/10-reasons-why-porn-is -unhealthy-for-consumers-and-society/.

22. "Pornography & Public Health Research Summary," National Center on Sexual Exploitation.

23. "Pornography," Enough Is Enough, accessed September 22, 2022, https://enough.org/stats _porn_industry.

24. "Statement: TEXXXAS Creator Claims Event Harmless, Research Shows Otherwise," National Center on Sexual Exploitation, July 25, 2016, https://endsexualexploitation .org/articles/statement-texxxas-creator -claims-event-harmless-research-shows -otherwise/#_edn4.

25. Hope for the Sold, "Connections between Porn, Prostitution & Trafficking," YouTube, video, 5:23, July 8, 2015, https://www.youtube .com/watch?v=iTh-Crp1aQs.

26. Robert W. Peters, Laura J. Lederer, and Shane Kelly, "The Slave and the Porn Star: Sexual Trafficking and Pornography," The Protection Project: Journal of Human Rights and Civil Society, Fall 2012, https://www.rescuefreedom .org/wp-content/uploads/2017/10/slave-and -the-porn-star.pdf.

27. Melissa Farley et al., "Comparing Sex Buyers with Men Who Do Not Buy Sex: New Data on Prostitution and Trafficking," *Journal of Interpersonal Violence* (2015) quoted at "Pornography & Public Health: Research Summary," Family First NZ, April 12, 2017, https://familyfirst.org.nz/2017/04/12 /pornography-public-health-research -summary/.

28. "Human Trafficking & Pornography," U.S. Catholic Sisters against Human Trafficking, accessed October 3, 2022, http://www.ipjc.org/wp-content/uploads/2016/09/USCSAHT%20-%20HT%20and%20Pornography%20module.pdf.

29. Keller and Dance, "Images of Child Sexual Abuse."

30. John Paul II, *Man and Woman: He Created Them: A Theology of the Body*, trans. Michael Waldstein (Boston: Pauline Books & Media, 2006).

31. Sean McDowell, "8 Inconvenient Truths about Pornography," SeanMcDowell.org, June 16, 2017, https://seanmcdowell.org/blog/7-inconvenient-truths-about-pornography.

32. Kristen A. Jenson, "6 Ways Savvy Kids Can Circumvent Your Internet Controls," Defend Young Minds, June 8, 2012, https://www.defendyoungminds.com/post/6-ways-savvy-kids-can-circumvent-your-internet-controls?share=twitter.

33. John Herrman, "How To: Hide Your 'Collection,'" Gizmodo, March 20, 2010,

https://gizmodo.com/how-to-hide-your
-collection-5497953.

34. Mike Wehner, "How to Hide Porn on Your
iPhone," Daily Dot, January 19, 2015, https://
www.dailydot.com/debug/iphone-porn/.

35. Marilyn Evans, "7 Signs a Child Is Viewing
Porn That Parents Often Overlook," Defend
Young Minds, November 2, 2017, https://www
.defendyoungminds.com/post/7-signs-child
-viewing-porn.

36. Patricia M. Greenfield, "Inadvertent Exposure
to Pornography on the Internet: Implications
of Peer-to-Peer File-Sharing Networks for
Child Development and Families," *Applied
Developmental Psychology* 25 (2004): 741–50,
https://www.sjsu.edu/people/carol
.mukhopadhyay/courses/AnthBioHS140/s6
/Greenfield-article-on-Porno-impacts.pdf.

37. "The SMART Plan Guide for Parents:
Helping Kids Who Have Been Exposed to
Pornography," Defend Young Minds, accessed
October 3, 2022, https://crossroadsgrace.
org/wp-content/uploads/sites/5/2021/01
/Protect-Young-Minds-SMART-Plan-for
-Parents-2019.pdf.

38. Kristen A. Jenson, "5 Reasons You Should Initiate Your Kid's Curiosity about Porn (Before Someone Else Does!)," Defend Young Minds, May 28, 2015, https:// www.defendyoungminds.com/post/ communication-counters-curiosity-5-reasons -you-should-initiate-the-talk-about-porn -before-someone-else-does.

39. "How Christian Parents Can Talk to Their Children about Sex," Seattle Christian Counseling, July 24, 2013, https:// seattlechristiancounseling.com/articles/how -christian-parents-can-talk-to-their-children -about-sex.

40. Christie Tate, "When to Talk to Kids about Internet Porn? Sooner Than Parents Think," *Washington Post*, October 9, 2017, https:// www.washingtonpost.com/news/parenting /wp/2017/10/09/when-should-parents-talk -to-kids-about-internet-pornography -sooner-than-they-think/.

41. "The Hard-to-Have Conversations: Talking with Your Child about Tricky Personal Subjects," eSafety Commissioner, Australian Government, https://www.esafety.gov.au /parents/skills-advice/hard-to-have -conversations.

42. "Porn in the Digital Age: New Research Reveals 10 Trends," Barna, April 6, 2016, https://www.barna.com/research/porn-in-the-digital-age-new-research-reveals-10-trends/.

PARENT GUIDES TO SOCIAL MEDIA
BY AXIS

It's common to feel lost in your teen's world. Let these be your go-to guides on social media, how it affects your teen, and how to begin an ongoing conversation about faith that matters.

BUNDLE THESE 5 BOOKS AND SAVE

DISCOVER MORE PARENT GUIDES, VIDEOS, AND AUDIOS AT AXIS.ORG

axis
www.axis.org

CP1805

PARENT GUIDES TO FINDING TRUE IDENTITY
BY AXIS

When culture is constantly pulling teens away from Christian values, let these five parent guides spark an ongoing conversation about finding your true identity in Christ.

BUNDLE THESE 5 BOOKS AND SAVE

DISCOVER MORE PARENT GUIDES, VIDEOS, AND AUDIOS AT AXIS.ORG

www.axis.org

CP1814

PARENT GUIDES TO MENTAL & SEXUAL HEALTH
BY AXIS

Don't let main-stream media be the only voice in your teens' conversations about mental and sexual health. Gain confidence and unravel your fears about breaching these sensitive topics today.

BUNDLE THESE 5 BOOKS AND SAVE

DISCOVER MORE PARENT GUIDES, VIDEOS, AND AUDIOS AT AXIS.ORG

www.axis.org

CP1846